★ THE ★
**UNITED
STATES**
PRESIDENTS

DWIGHT D.
EISENHOWER

Tamara L. Britton

**Checkerboard
Library**

An Imprint of Abdo Publishing
abdobooks.com

ABDOBOOKS.COM

Published by Abdo Publishing, a division of ABDO, PO Box 398166, Minneapolis, Minnesota 55439. Copyright © 2021 by Abdo Consulting Group, Inc. International copyrights reserved in all countries. No part of this book may be reproduced in any form without written permission from the publisher. Checkerboard Library™ is a trademark and logo of Abdo Publishing.

Printed in the United States of America, North Mankato, Minnesota
052020
092020

THIS BOOK CONTAINS RECYCLED MATERIALS

Design: Emily O'Malley, Kelly Doudna, Mighty Media, Inc.
Production: Mighty Media, Inc.
Editor: Liz Salzmann

Cover Photograph: Getty Images
Interior Photographs: Albert de Bruijn/iStockphoto, p. 37; AP Images, pp. 6, 7 (General Eisenhower), 11, 12, 18, 19, 21, 30, 31, 36; Express/Getty Images, p. 20; Getty Images, pp. 5, 13, 14, 17, 29; James P. Blair/Getty Images, p. 33; Library of Congress, pp. 27, 40; Mark Kauffman/Getty Images, p. 25; MPI/Getty Images, p. 23; P&P/Library of Congress, p. 24; Pete Souza/Flickr, p. 44; Shutterstock Images, pp. 15, 38, 39; Wikimedia Commons, pp. 7, 40 (George Washington), 42

Library of Congress Control Number: 2019956446

Publisher's Cataloging-in-Publication Data
Names: Britton, Tamara L., author.
Title: Dwight D. Eisenhower / by Tamara L. Britton
Description: Minneapolis, Minnesota : Abdo Publishing, 2021 | Series: The United States presidents | Includes online resources and index.
Identifiers: ISBN 9781532193477 (lib. bdg.) | ISBN 9781098212117 (ebook)
Subjects: LCSH: Eisenhower, Dwight D. (Dwight David), 1890-1969--Juvenile literature. | Presidents—Biography--Juvenile literature. | Presidents--United States--History--Juvenile literature. | Legislators—United States--Biography--Juvenile literature. | Politics and government--Biography--Juvenile literature.
Classification: DDC 973.921092--dc23

★ CONTENTS ★

Dwight D. Eisenhower

General Dwight D. Eisenhower was one of the most successful military leaders in US history. He commanded the **Allies** in Europe during **World War II**. When the war ended, Eisenhower continued on in the military as the army **chief of staff**. Later, he became the first head of **NATO** forces.

In 1952, Eisenhower easily defeated Adlai E. Stevenson II in the presidential election. Eisenhower took office in January 1953. He was the first **Republican** president in 20 years.

Under Eisenhower's leadership, businesses did well. Most Americans had jobs. And, Eisenhower met with world leaders to make peace.

Americans liked President Eisenhower and the way he ran the country. He had an easygoing personality and a cheerful grin. He was an honorable man.

★ TIMELINE ★

1890

Dwight David Eisenhower was born on October 14 in Denison, Texas.

1915

Eisenhower graduated from the US Military Academy at West Point in New York.

1933

Eisenhower became General Douglas MacArthur's assistant.

1943

Eisenhower was named supreme commander of the Allied Expeditionary Force in Europe.

1916

On July 1, Eisenhower married Mary "Mamie" Doud.

1941

The United States entered World War II.

1942

Eisenhower was transferred to London, England, to command US forces in Europe. Eisenhower was in charge of the invasion of North Africa.

1944

Operation Overlord began on June 6. Eisenhower was named a five-star general on December 20.

1957

Congress approved the Eisenhower Doctrine. Eisenhower sent the US Army's 101st Airborne unit to Little Rock Central High School in Little Rock, Arkansas. Eisenhower signed the Civil Rights Act of 1957. The Soviets launched *Sputnik I*.

1945

The war ended in Europe on May 8. Eisenhower was named army chief of staff.

1948

Eisenhower retired from the army. He became president of Columbia University.

1953

On January 20, Eisenhower became the thirty-fourth president.

1956

Eisenhower was reelected US president.

1969

Dwight D. Eisenhower died on March 28.

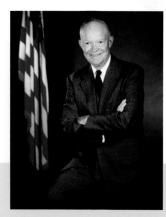

"In the councils of government, **we must guard against the acquisition of unwarranted influence,** whether sought or unsought, by the military-industrial complex."

DWIGHT D. EISENHOWER

DID YOU KNOW?

★ President Dwight D. Eisenhower believed that new, multilane highways would aid in national defense. On June 29, 1956, he signed the Federal Aid Highway Act. It created the Eisenhower Interstate Highway system.

★ President Franklin D. Roosevelt built a presidential retreat in Maryland. He named it Shangri-La. President Eisenhower later renamed the retreat Camp David after his grandson.

★ Alaska officially became the forty-ninth state on January 3, 1959. On August 21, 1959, Hawaii became the fiftieth state. President Eisenhower was the first president to govern all 50 states.

★ Eisenhower's full name was David Dwight Eisenhower. However, he was called Dwight so he wouldn't be confused with his father. Later in life, Eisenhower officially changed his name to Dwight David.

Young Dwight

Dwight David Eisenhower was born on October 14, 1890, in Denison, Texas. His parents were David and Ida Eisenhower. The Eisenhowers raised six sons. They were Dwight, Arthur, Edgar, Roy, Earl, and Milton.

The Eisenhowers moved to Abilene, Kansas, when Dwight was less than two years old. Dwight's friends called him Ike. The nickname stayed with him his whole life.

Ike was a good student. He did well in English, history, and geometry. He was a friendly person and a good athlete. In high school, Ike played both baseball and football.

Ike graduated from Abilene High School in 1909. For the next two years, he worked to help his family. The money Ike made allowed his brother Edgar to attend college.

Since his family didn't have much money, Ike decided to

FAST FACTS

BORN: October 14, 1890

WIFE: Mary "Mamie" Doud (1896–1979)

CHILDREN: 2

POLITICAL PARTY: Republican

AGE AT INAUGURATION: 62

YEARS SERVED: 1953–1961

VICE PRESIDENT: Richard Nixon

DIED: March 28, 1969, age 78

Dwight (*far left*) with his family

attend military school. In 1911, he entered the US Military Academy at West Point in New York. There, his education would be free. And, he could play on the academy's football team.

College and Marriage

Eisenhower loved playing football at West Point. He was an excellent player. But, he hurt his knee during his second year. The injury ended his football career forever. It was a crushing blow. Eisenhower had trouble adjusting to life without football.

The Eisenhowers in 1918, soon after their marriage

In college, Eisenhower was an average student. He often got in trouble for breaking the rules. Still, he graduated from West Point in 1915. Eisenhower was sixty-first in his class of 164 students. After graduation, he became a second lieutenant in the US Army.

Eisenhower's first military assignment was at Fort Sam Houston in Texas. On a weekend off, he went to nearby San Antonio. There, he met Mary "Mamie" Doud. On July 1, 1916, the two married. That same day, Eisenhower was promoted to first lieutenant.

In 1917, the Eisenhowers welcomed their first child. They named him Doud but called him Icky. When he was only three years old, Icky became ill and died. For the rest of his life, Eisenhower sent his wife flowers on Icky's birthday.

The Eisenhowers with their son Doud

Military Man

Eisenhower was promoted to captain in 1917. He wanted to go to Europe to fight in **World War I**. But army officials believed he could better serve by training new soldiers. So in 1918, Eisenhower was named head of Camp Colt. This was a training base in Gettysburg, Pennsylvania. Eisenhower was promoted to major in 1920. He later received the Distinguished Service Medal for his service during the war.

In 1922, Eisenhower was sent to the **Panama Canal** Zone to protect the new canal. Mrs. Eisenhower disliked the conditions in Panama. So, she often stayed in Denver, Colorado, with her family. There, the Eisenhowers welcomed a second son named John.

To advance his career, Eisenhower attended the Command and General Staff School in Leavenworth, Kansas. There, he

MacArthur (*left*) and Eisenhower

The Panama Canal opened on August 15, 1914.

was a hardworking student. This time, he graduated first in his class of 275 students.

The army recognized Eisenhower as an outstanding officer. In 1933, he became General Douglas MacArthur's assistant. Eisenhower helped MacArthur develop a defense plan in the Philippines.

Eisenhower had a successful career in the army. But he was unsatisfied. Eisenhower wanted to command troops. **World War II** soon provided him this opportunity.

World War II

In 1941, the United States entered **World War II**. Eisenhower was promoted to colonel and then brigadier general. The next year, he moved up to major general and then lieutenant general. In 1942, his hard work paid off. He was transferred to London, England, to command US forces in Europe.

General Eisenhower was in charge of the invasion of North Africa in July 1942. American forces planned to move east to meet British forces that were moving west from Egypt.

Eisenhower's men met early defeats. Then, Eisenhower put General George Patton in charge. After seven months, the Americans met up with the British and defeated the Germans. This victory earned Eisenhower a promotion to four-star general.

Army officials recognized Eisenhower's talent for getting different groups to cooperate and reach a common goal. So in 1943, Eisenhower was named supreme commander of the **Allied** Expeditionary Force in Europe. In this role,

Allied forces meet in North Africa

he would carry out Operation Overlord. This was the code name for an invasion of Western Europe.

On June 6, 1944, the **Allies** landed in Normandy, France. This is known as D-day. In six days, the beach was secured. The Germans fled east across Europe. On August 25, the **Allies** freed Paris, France, from German control. Then, the Allies forced the Germans all the way back to Germany. Operation Overlord was one of the greatest operations in military history. Because of its success, Eisenhower was

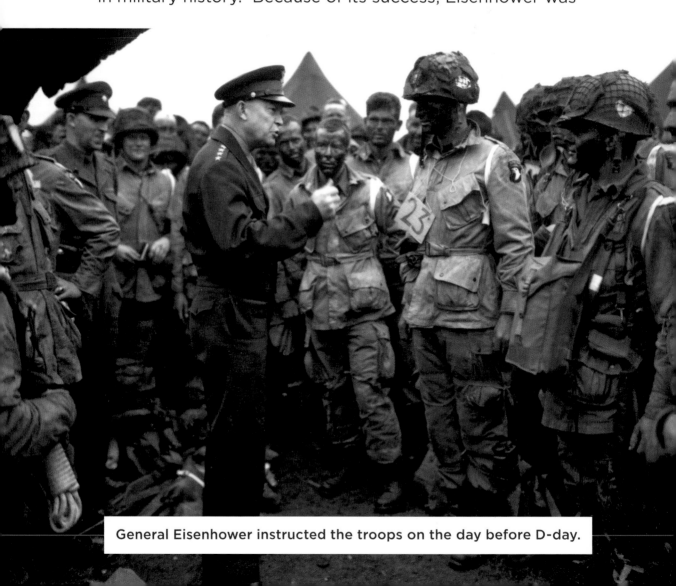

General Eisenhower instructed the troops on the day before D-day.

President Eisenhower (*left*) reviewed South Korean troops during his visit.

Pittsburgh, Pennsylvania, discovered a drug to stop **polio**. Millions of people had suffered from this disease.

President Eisenhower worked with Secretary of Health and Human Services Oveta Culp Hobby. Together, they came up with a plan to give the drug to Americans. Today, polio has almost been erased in the United States.

On September 24, 1955, President Eisenhower and the whole country suffered a scare. While on vacation in Colorado, he had a heart attack. It was a few months before the president fully recovered.

In December, President Eisenhower was ready to return to work. Many Americans wondered if he would run for a second term. Eisenhower told the nation he would run for reelection.

President and Mrs. Eisenhower held a picnic to mark the start of the reelection campaign.

Oveta Culp Hobby (*above*) was only the second woman to serve on a president's cabinet. The first was Frances Perkins, President Franklin D. Roosevelt's secretary of labor.

PRESIDENT EISENHOWER'S CABINET

FIRST TERM

January 20, 1953–January 20, 1957

- ★ **STATE:** John Foster Dulles
- ★ **TREASURY:** George M. Humphrey
- ★ **DEFENSE:** Charles E. Wilson
- ★ **ATTORNEY GENERAL:** Herbert Brownell Jr.
- ★ **INTERIOR:** Douglas McKay
  Frederick A. Seaton (from June 8, 1956)
- ★ **AGRICULTURE:** Ezra Taft Benson
- ★ **COMMERCE:** Sinclair Weeks
- ★ **LABOR:** Martin P. Durkin
  James P. Mitchell (from October 9, 1953)
- ★ **HEALTH, EDUCATION, AND WELFARE:**
  Oveta Culp Hobby (from April 11, 1953)
  Marion B. Folsom (from August 1, 1955)

SECOND TERM

January 20, 1957–January 20, 1961

- ★ **STATE:** John Foster Dulles
  Christian A. Herter (from April 22, 1959)
- ★ **TREASURY:** George M. Humphrey
  Robert B. Anderson (from July 29, 1957)
- ★ **DEFENSE:** Charles E. Wilson
  Neil H. McElroy (from October 9, 1957)
  Thomas S. Gates Jr. (from December 2, 1959)
- ★ **ATTORNEY GENERAL:** Herbert Brownell Jr.
  William P. Rogers (from January 27, 1958)
- ★ **INTERIOR:** Frederick A. Seaton
- ★ **AGRICULTURE:** Ezra Taft Benson
- ★ **COMMERCE:** Sinclair Weeks
  Frederick H. Mueller (from August 10, 1959)
- ★ **LABOR:** James P. Mitchell
- ★ **HEALTH, EDUCATION, AND WELFARE:**
  Marion B. Folsom
  Arthur S. Flemming (from August 1, 1958)

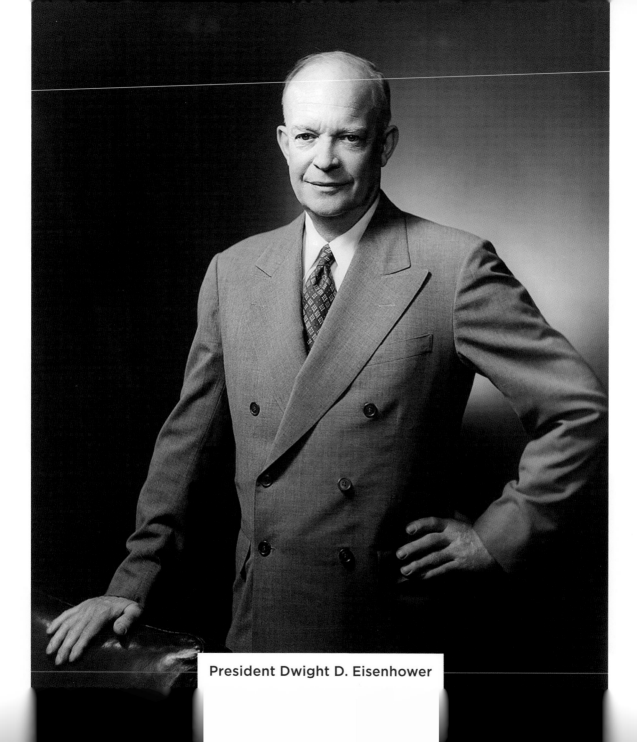

President Dwight D. Eisenhower

8

A Second Term

In 1956, the **Democrats** again chose Adlai E. Stevenson II as their presidential candidate. In this election, his **running mate** was Senator Estes Kefauver of Tennessee. President Eisenhower and Vice President Nixon ran on the **Republican** ticket.

In November, Eisenhower and Nixon were easily reelected. But Eisenhower faced problems both at home and abroad. In 1954, President Eisenhower had signed the Communist Control Act. This made the Communist Party in the United States unlawful.

People in other parts of the world were also worried about the spread of Communism. President Eisenhower asked Congress for money to help any Middle Eastern nation that wanted to fight its spread. Congress approved this plan in March 1957. It became known as the Eisenhower Doctrine.

At home, it was a difficult time in US history. Protests were going on throughout the country. African Americans and their supporters were fighting for **civil rights**.

In the South, many people wanted separate schools for white and black children. They also wanted separate water fountains and restaurants. African Americans were forced to sit in the backs of buses. And, laws were passed to keep them from voting.

There was also resistance to the *Brown v. Board of Education of Topeka* ruling. In September 1957, nine African American students were enrolled at Little Rock Central High School in Little Rock, Arkansas. Mobs of white people tried to keep the children from entering the school building. Governor Orval Faubus sent the Arkansas **National Guard** to keep the students out of school.

Elizabeth Eckford (*front*) was one of the nine African American students enrolled in Central High School. She had to walk to class amid taunts from white students.

As president, Eisenhower's job was to protect and defend the US **Constitution**. He sent the US Army's 101st Airborne unit to protect the children's constitutional rights. The soldiers made sure the children were allowed into the school. The children had military protection for the entire school year.

That same year, Eisenhower signed the **Civil Rights** Act of 1957. The law increased protection of voting rights. It also created the Civil Rights Commission.

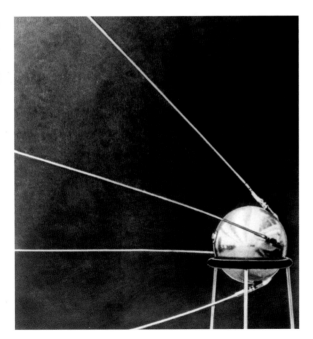

— The official photograph of *Sputnik I* released on October 9, 1957, showed the first man-made object to orbit the earth.

That same year, the Soviet Union put the first **satellite** into space. They launched *Sputnik I* on October 4, 1957. So in 1958, President Eisenhower asked Congress to create a space agency. The organization would research and explore the universe. Congress approved Eisenhower's plan. The National Aeronautics and Space Administration was formed.

Government officials were concerned about Soviet intentions. They wanted to see if the Soviets had more **missiles** than the United States. So, air force pilots flew spy airplanes over the Soviet Union.

On May 1, 1960, the Soviets shot down one of the spy airplanes. They captured its pilot, Francis Gary Powers. Eisenhower then had to admit the United States was spying.

Khrushchev (*left*) visited Eisenhower in the United States in 1959. The spy airplane incident obstructed Eisenhower's efforts to improve relations between the two nations.

As a result, Soviet leader Nikita Khrushchev refused to attend a meeting to discuss reducing weapons production. President Eisenhower was disappointed. He had seen the horrors of war. He regretted that he could not do more to protect future generations from its effects.

9

Home at Last

On February 27, 1951, a new **amendment** had been added to the US **Constitution**. The Twenty-second Amendment said that no one could be president for more than two terms. Eisenhower was the first president required by this new law to leave the White House.

January 20, 1961, was Eisenhower's last day as president. That day, John F. Kennedy took office. He had defeated Vice President Richard Nixon to become the new president.

Eisenhower retired to his farm in Gettysburg, Pennsylvania. He raised animals and played golf. He also spent time with his family and wrote his **memoirs**.

Throughout 1968, Eisenhower's health worsened. He was in the hospital for almost a year. Then on March 28, 1969, Dwight D. Eisenhower died of heart failure.

Many world leaders and everyday citizens came to the Capitol to pay their respects to Eisenhower. At the time of Eisenhower's death, former vice president Richard Nixon was president. Nixon gave a speech in which he revealed some of Eisenhower's last words. Eisenhower had said,

Eisenhower was buried in Abilene, Kansas,
in the chapel at the Eisenhower Center.

"I've always loved my wife. I've always loved my children.
I've always loved my grandchildren. I've always loved my
country."

BRANCHES OF GOVERNMENT

The US government is divided into three branches. They are the executive, legislative, and judicial branches. This division is called a separation of powers. Each branch has some power over the others. This is called a system of checks and balances.

★ EXECUTIVE BRANCH

The executive branch enforces laws. It is made up of the president, the vice president, and the president's cabinet. The president represents the United States around the world. He or she oversees relations with other countries and signs treaties. The president signs bills into law and appoints officials and federal judges. He or she also leads the military and manages government workers.

★ LEGISLATIVE BRANCH

The legislative branch makes laws, maintains the military, and regulates trade. It also has the power to declare war. This branch consists of the Senate and the House of Representatives. Together, these two houses make up Congress. Each state has two senators. A state's population determines the number of representatives it has.

★ JUDICIAL BRANCH

The judicial branch interprets laws. It consists of district courts, courts of appeals, and the Supreme Court. District courts try cases. If a person disagrees with a trial's outcome, he or she may appeal. If a court of appeals supports the ruling, a person may appeal to the Supreme Court. The Supreme Court also makes sure that laws follow the US Constitution.

THE PRESIDENT ★

★ QUALIFICATIONS FOR OFFICE

To be president, a person must meet three requirements. A candidate must be at least 35 years old and a natural-born US citizen. He or she must also have lived in the United States for at least 14 years.

★ ELECTORAL COLLEGE

The US presidential election is an indirect election. Voters from each state choose electors to represent them in the Electoral College. The number of electors from each state is based on the state's population. Each elector has one electoral vote. Electors are pledged to cast their vote for the candidate who receives the highest number of popular votes in their state. A candidate must receive the majority of Electoral College votes to win.

★ TERM OF OFFICE

Each president may be elected to two four-year terms. Sometimes, a president may only be elected once. This happens if he or she served more than two years of the previous president's term.

The presidential election is held on the Tuesday after the first Monday in November. The president is sworn in on January 20 of the following year. At that time, he or she takes the oath of office:

> *I do solemnly swear (or affirm) that I will faithfully execute the office of President of the United States, and will to the best of my ability, preserve, protect and defend the Constitution of the United States.*

LINE OF SUCCESSION

The Presidential Succession Act of 1947 defines who becomes president if the president cannot serve. The vice president is first in the line of succession. Next are the Speaker of the House and the President Pro Tempore of the Senate. If none of these individuals is able to serve, the office falls to the president's cabinet members. They would take office in the order in which each department was created:

Secretary of State

Secretary of the Treasury

Secretary of Defense

Attorney General

Secretary of the Interior

Secretary of Agriculture

Secretary of Commerce

Secretary of Labor

Secretary of Health and Human Services

Secretary of Housing and Urban Development

Secretary of Transportation

Secretary of Energy

Secretary of Education

Secretary of Veterans Affairs

Secretary of Homeland Security

While in office, the president receives a salary of $400,000 each year. He or she lives in the White House and has 24-hour Secret Service protection.

The president may travel on a Boeing 747 jet called Air Force One. The airplane can accommodate 76 passengers. It has kitchens, a dining room, sleeping areas, and a conference room. It also has fully equipped offices with the latest communications systems. Air Force One can fly halfway around the world before needing to refuel. It can even refuel in flight!

Air Force One

If the president wishes to travel by car, he or she uses Cadillac One. It has been modified with heavy armor and communications systems. The president takes

Cadillac One along when visiting other countries if secure transportation will be needed.

The president also travels on a helicopter called Marine One. Like the presidential car, Marine One accompanies the president when traveling abroad if necessary.

Cadillac One

Sometimes, the president needs to get away and relax with family and friends. Camp David is the official presidential retreat. It is located in the cool, wooded mountains of Maryland. The US Navy maintains the retreat, and the US Marine Corps keeps it secure. The camp offers swimming, tennis, golf, and hiking.

When the president leaves office, he or she receives lifetime Secret Service protection. He or she also receives a yearly pension of $207,800 and funding for office space, supplies, and staff.

Marine One

George Washington

Abraham Lincoln

Theodore Roosevelt

	PRESIDENT	PARTY	TOOK OFFICE
1	George Washington	None	April 30, 1789
2	John Adams	Federalist	March 4, 1797
3	Thomas Jefferson	Democratic-Republican	March 4, 1801
4	James Madison	Democratic-Republican	March 4, 1809
5	James Monroe	Democratic-Republican	March 4, 1817
6	John Quincy Adams	Democratic-Republican	March 4, 1825
7	Andrew Jackson	Democrat	March 4, 1829
8	Martin Van Buren	Democrat	March 4, 1837
9	William H. Harrison	Whig	March 4, 1841
10	John Tyler	Whig	April 6, 1841
11	James K. Polk	Democrat	March 4, 1845
12	Zachary Taylor	Whig	March 5, 1849
13	Millard Fillmore	Whig	July 10, 1850
14	Franklin Pierce	Democrat	March 4, 1853
15	James Buchanan	Democrat	March 4, 1857
16	Abraham Lincoln	Republican	March 4, 1861
17	Andrew Johnson	Democrat	April 15, 1865
18	Ulysses S. Grant	Republican	March 4, 1869
19	Rutherford B. Hayes	Republican	March 3, 1877

LEFT OFFICE	TERMS SERVED	VICE PRESIDENT
March 4, 1797	Two	John Adams
March 4, 1801	One	Thomas Jefferson
March 4, 1809	Two	Aaron Burr, George Clinton
March 4, 1817	Two	George Clinton, Elbridge Gerry
March 4, 1825	Two	Daniel D. Tompkins
March 4, 1829	One	John C. Calhoun
March 4, 1837	Two	John C. Calhoun, Martin Van Buren
March 4, 1841	One	Richard M. Johnson
April 4, 1841	Died During First Term	John Tyler
March 4, 1845	Completed Harrison's Term	Office Vacant
March 4, 1849	One	George M. Dallas
July 9, 1850	Died During First Term	Millard Fillmore
March 4, 1853	Completed Taylor's Term	Office Vacant
March 4, 1857	One	William R.D. King
March 4, 1861	One	John C. Breckinridge
April 15, 1865	Served One Term, Died During Second Term	Hannibal Hamlin, Andrew Johnson
March 4, 1869	Completed Lincoln's Second Term	Office Vacant
March 4, 1877	Two	Schuyler Colfax, Henry Wilson
March 4, 1881	One	William A. Wheeler

Franklin D. Roosevelt

John F. Kennedy

Ronald Reagan

	PRESIDENT	PARTY	TOOK OFFICE
20	James A. Garfield	Republican	March 4, 1881
21	Chester Arthur	Republican	September 20, 1881
22	Grover Cleveland	Democrat	March 4, 1885
23	Benjamin Harrison	Republican	March 4, 1889
24	Grover Cleveland	Democrat	March 4, 1893
25	William McKinley	Republican	March 4, 1897
26	Theodore Roosevelt	Republican	September 14, 1901
27	William Taft	Republican	March 4, 1909
28	Woodrow Wilson	Democrat	March 4, 1913
29	Warren G. Harding	Republican	March 4, 1921
30	Calvin Coolidge	Republican	August 3, 1923
31	Herbert Hoover	Republican	March 4, 1929
32	Franklin D. Roosevelt	Democrat	March 4, 1933
33	Harry S. Truman	Democrat	April 12, 1945
34	Dwight D. Eisenhower	Republican	January 20, 1953
35	John F. Kennedy	Democrat	January 20, 1961

LEFT OFFICE	TERMS SERVED	VICE PRESIDENT
September 19, 1881	Died During First Term	Chester Arthur
March 4, 1885	Completed Garfield's Term	Office Vacant
March 4, 1889	One	Thomas A. Hendricks
March 4, 1893	One	Levi P. Morton
March 4, 1897	One	Adlai E. Stevenson
September 14, 1901	Served One Term, Died During Second Term	Garret A. Hobart, Theodore Roosevelt
March 4, 1909	Completed McKinley's Second Term, Served One Term	Office Vacant, Charles Fairbanks
March 4, 1913	One	James S. Sherman
March 4, 1921	Two	Thomas R. Marshall
August 2, 1923	Died During First Term	Calvin Coolidge
March 4, 1929	Completed Harding's Term, Served One Term	Office Vacant, Charles Dawes
March 4, 1933	One	Charles Curtis
April 12, 1945	Served Three Terms, Died During Fourth Term	John Nance Garner, Henry A. Wallace, Harry S. Truman
January 20, 1953	Completed Roosevelt's Fourth Term, Served One Term	Office Vacant, Alben Barkley
January 20, 1961	Two	Richard Nixon
November 22, 1963	Died During First Term	Lyndon B. Johnson

	PRESIDENT	PARTY	TOOK OFFICE
36	Lyndon B. Johnson	Democrat	November 22, 1963
37	Richard Nixon	Republican	January 20, 1969
38	Gerald Ford	Republican	August 9, 1974
39	Jimmy Carter	Democrat	January 20, 1977
40	Ronald Reagan	Republican	January 20, 1981
41	George H.W. Bush	Republican	January 20, 1989
42	Bill Clinton	Democrat	January 20, 1993
43	George W. Bush	Republican	January 20, 2001
44	Barack Obama	Democrat	January 20, 2009
45	Donald Trump	Republican	January 20, 2017

Barack Obama

★ PRESIDENTS MATH GAME ★

Have fun with this presidents math game! First, study the list above and memorize each president's name and number. Then, use math to figure out which president completes each equation below.

1. Dwight D. Eisenhower + Andrew Jackson = ?

2. John Quincy Adams + Dwight D. Eisenhower = ?

3. Lyndon B. Johnson – Dwight D. Eisenhower = ?

Answers: 1. George H.W. Bush (34 + 7 = 41)
2. Ronald Reagan (6 + 34 = 40)
3. John Adams (36 – 34 = 2)